CAMP FUN!

100+ SUMMER CAMP GAMES, JOKES, ACTIVITIES AND CHALLENGES FOR CAMPERS AND THEIR FRIENDS

BEX BAND

CONTENTS

Camp Fun! v

1. Summer Camp Fillers 1
2. Would You Rather? Summer Camp Edition 26
3. Summer Camp Jokes 41
4. Summer Camp Writing Journal Prompts 48
5. Small Group Games 52
6. Large Group Games 75
7. Campfire Riddles 97
   Riddle Answers 102
8. Campfire Conversations 105

CAMP FUN!

Welcome to the ultimate guide to summer camp fun!

I don't think I realised how much of a positive impact going on summer camps had on me until I was an adult.

As a child, my favourite memories were attending ATE Superweek summer camps in the UK (www.superweeks.co.uk). They were filled with fun, games, adventure and friendships, so it's no surprise I returned to work as a counsellor.

As an adult, I still craved the sense of adventure and community that I had found at summer camp, but I struggled to find it anywhere. So, I launched Love Her Wild (www.loveherwild.com)—a women's adventure community—and made going on adventures my job!

This book came about to share some of the best games, activities and conversation starters I've collected over the years. To help harness those small moments that make camp so special.

Whether you're a camper or a counsellor, this book is packed with awesome games, brain-teasing riddles, laugh-out-loud "Would You Rather" questions, and epic challenges to set for your friends.

FOR MORE OUTDOOR INSPIRATION AND TO FOLLOW MY ADVENTURES, FIND ME ON:

YouTube: @BandFamilyAdventures

Instagram: @Bex_Band

Facebook: @BexBand

CHAPTER 1
SUMMER CAMP FILLERS

Test yourself in between activities or while hanging out in your bunk-room with these challenges, quick games, riddles and teasers.

Some are designed to trick and confuse your friends!

Some require you to work as a team to solve the challenge!

And some will have you in fits of laughter!

THE LOOP

- Form a circle and hold hands.
- A hoop made of knotted rope or wool must be passed around the circle without anyone letting go.
- Participants cannot use their fingers to pass the hoop and must start over if anyone lets go.

BANG, BANG!

- Using their finger to gesture a gun, the leaser randomly points at people in the room, saying “bang, bang!”
- After which, the leader will ask, “who did I kill?”.
- Everyone makes guesses at who they think is now dead.
- Secret: The first person who speaks after the leader asks the question is considered "dead."
- See how long it takes everyone to work it out.

MY GRANNY DOESN'T LIKE TEA

- Say, “My granny likes coffee but she doesn’t like tea.”
- Players suggest things your granny might like or dislike.
- Secret: She dislikes anything with the letter “T” in it.

FRUIT CHARADES

- Take turns acting out a fruit or vegetable without speaking.
- The rest of the group guesses what the person is mimicking.

SHADOW PUPPETS

- Use torches, bed sheets, and hand shadows to create a story as a group or in separate teams.
- Organise a performance time to showcase the story to the rest of the group or camp.

STICKS CHALLENGE

- Give a child a large stick and ask them to balance it between their index fingers.
- Then, ask them to balance it with another person, both using one index finger each.
- Try balancing it on different body parts (elbows, knees) and once the players have got the hang of it, challenge them to move to a place nearby and back again without dropping the stick.

MEDITATION TRICK

- One staff member starts a meditation session with the group, doing some silly poses and having the children close their eyes.
- Another staff member signals the children to quietly leave the room to play games or participate in an outdoor activity.
- The meditating staff member can take a break but must return before the children return (quietly turning and taking their original places), pretending the meditation session lasted the entire time.

WOOPS BUNNY

- Using your fingers, say "bunny, bunny, bunny, bunny, woops bunny, woops, bunny, bunny, bunny, bunny" while making hand motions.
- Ask everyone to repeat the actions until everyone guesses the secret.
- Secret: They must cross their arms at the end to get it right.

MAGIC CUP

- Attach a plastic or foam cup to your thumb without anyone noticing using double-sided sticky tape.
- Place your hands around the cup without touching it, creating the illusion that the cup is floating in mid-air.

TOFFEE TWIN

- Each person secretly picks the name of another group member from a hat.
- The person whose name they draw is their Toffee Twin, and they must keep their identity secret.
- Every day while on camp, participants must do something nice for their Toffee Twin - it could be carrying a bag, giving them a slice of cake, making a compliment, organising a surprise for when they return to their bunk - the more creative the better. The

only rule is they must carry out the act without revealing their identity.

- At the end of camp, ask everyone to guess who their Toffee Twin is and why before everyone reveals who they really are.

GLUED TO A CHAIR

- One participant sits in a chair and tilts their head back so they are looking up.
- Another person stands behind them, placing a little finger on the sitter's forehead.
- The sitter tries to stand up while the other person uses their little finger to stop them. This task is surprisingly difficult!

QUICK-CHANGE ACT

- Get everyone who is playing to sit in a circle.
- Select one person to be "on".
- This person goes out of sight and changes something visible (e.g., puts shorts on backwards, changes hairstyle).
- They return and turn around slowly for everyone to see.
- The first person to correctly guess the change becomes the next person "on".

CHINESE WHISPERS

- Everyone sits in a circle and selects someone to start.
- This person thinks of a sentence and whispers it to the person on their left.
- Each player whispers what they heard to the next person only once.
- When the message reaches the last person, they stand up and say the sentence they heard.
- Typically, the sentence will have changed significantly.

---

20 QUESTIONS

- The person who is "on" first needs to thinks of either a famous person or an object (you can set boundaries for this - ie, it needs to be an object you'd find at summer camp or a famous actor)
- Once they've chosen, they announce, "I'm thinking of a person/object."
- Players take turns asking yes-or-no questions to guess the person or object.
- There are a total of 20 questions allowed.
- The player who guesses correctly goes next.
- If no one gets it right, the player reveals what they were thinking and then stays on, choosing a new person/object.

THE ONE-WORD STORY

- Someone starts with a word, for example, "once."
- The next person adds a word, like "a."
- The story continues with each person adding a word without pausing to think.
- The goal is to keep the story flowing without hesitation.

GEOGRAPHY GAME

- One person names a country, such as China.
- The next person names a country starting with the last letter of the previous country, like Argentina following China.
- This can also be played with animals, names of people, or other categories.

THE ALPHABET GAME

- The aim is to find all the letters of the alphabet in order, from A to Z.
- Letters can be spotted anywhere, but once a player claims a letter, others cannot use it.
- The first person to complete the alphabet wins.

I'M PACKING A BAG

- A player begins by stating, "I'm going to summer camp and I'm packing a bag. I pack a..." followed by an item they might take to camp, such as pyjamas. The items can also be silly, such as slime.
- The next player repeats the same sentence, including what the player before decided to pack, and then adds another item to the bag.
- The game continues with each player recalling all previously mentioned items and adding a new one.
- The game can also be played with a shopping trolley instead of a suitcase.

ANIMAL NOISES

- One person is blindfolded and stands in the centre of the room.
- Everyone else walks around the blindfolded person in a circle.
- The person in the middle shouts "stop" and points to someone in the circle, then names an animal.
- The chosen person must make the sound of that animal.
- If the blindfolded person guesses who made the noise, they swap places; otherwise, the game continues.

2 STRAW TEASE

- Take a glass of water and two straws.
- Place both straws in your mouth, but only one in the water and the other outside.

- No matter how hard you suck, you won't be able to get any water through the straw.

MYSTERY NAPKIN

- Stick a fork into a potato and cover it with a napkin or cloth.
- Move the fork up and down, making it look like the napkin is coming to life.

IMPOSSIBLY STRONG

- Tell the group you have incredible strength.
- Point both of your index fingers towards each other until they are touching.
- Challenge a friend to hold your wrists and try to pull your fingers apart. It will be very difficult for them!

THE BROOM CHALLENGE

- Have a participant crouch with a broom handle (or a long straight stick) behind their knees and elbows.
- Place an object on the floor and challenge them to pick it up without dropping the sticks.

MAGIC PENCIL TRICK

- Hold one hand flat in front of you. In your other hand, hold a pencil between your thumb and finger.
- Tell everyone to keep a close eye on your flat hand as it's magic and can make things disappear. Move the pencil back and forth in an upward motion from your flat hand to over your shoulder.
- On one of the upward motions, tuck the pencil behind your ear, before bringing your hand down hard on your flat hand. This gives the impression the pencil has just disappeared! (You'll want to practice this motion in advance so it's smooth when you do it in front of your friends).
- Then repeat the motions and make the pencil reappear by taking it from behind your ear in a swift movement.

FINGER CIRCLES

- Challenge someone to point their two index fingers towards each other.
- Now tell them rotate one finger clockwise, while the other finger rotates counterclockwise.
- This is nearly impossible!

DON'T SAY YES

- Choose someone to be "on."
- Everyone else tries to get this person to say the word "yes."

- If they do, the person who tricked them successfully into saying “yes” becomes "on."

BUILDING BLOCKS

- Arrange four chairs in a square and have four participants sit sideways.
- Tell them to lean back until they are lying flat on someone else's legs and have someone lying on their own legs.
- Remove the chairs, and the participants should remain supported by each other’s weight.

DRAWING

- The leader needs to have a stick or pen in their hand. Using the stick or pen, dram the shape of a moon crescent in the air (you may want to confuse your camper friends by adding detail to your drawing, such as eyes or stars).
- Pass the stick/pen around, instructing everyone to copy you, saying if they’ve done it correctly or not.
- They are correct only if they say “thank you” when the stick is passed to them! See how long it takes for your friends to work it out.

UNSTABLE

- This is a really cool trick to do with your friend - it'll blow their mind!
- Get them to lie belly down on the floor with their arms stretched out above their head.
- Grabbing both their arms with your hands, lift their arms until their upper body is off the floor. It's important their head stays relaxed and floppy so it hangs down between their arms.
- Hold this position for a minute (keep reminding the participant to keep their head relaxed because they'll want to instinctively hold it up)
- Very slowly, they lower their arms towards the ground. Their heads will be the first thing to touch the floor.
- When this happens, and their arms continue moving down, it gives them the feeling that their hands are going through the floor.

GLUED

- Have a participant stand with their left shoulder and left foot flat against a wall.
- Tell them to lift their right leg. This is an impossible challenge because they are unbalanced.

IN MY BACKPACK

- The first player says, "In my backpack there is..." and adds an item.

- The next player repeats the sentence and adds another item.
- Continue around the circle, adding new items each time.
- If a player gets the sequence wrong, they are out.

IT'S ONLY PICKING UP A CHAIR

- Place a chair against a wall.
- Have a participant stand in front of it and lean forward so their forehead rests on the wall.
- Tell them to pick up the chair with both hands and then stand up straight without letting go. This is much harder than it sounds!

COIN TRICK

- Tell your friend that you are going to challenge them, but will first demonstrate what they need to do.
- Taking a coin, push it firmly into the middle of your forehead, between your eyes. After a few seconds, it will stick and stay in place once you've let go.
- Leaning your head forward, hit the back of your head. This will cause a knock and the coin to fall off your head and into your hand.
- Ask a participant if they want to try. Help them press the coin into their forehead but then sneakily remove the coin (to them it will still feel like it's attached).
- Watch them tap their head, thinking the coin is still there!

TREE RUBBING

- Use wax crayons to create rubbings of tree bark.
- Use different colours for seasonal effects and cut the paper into leaf shapes for decorating your cabin.

GOING TO ITALY

- Players sit in a circle. The Leader says, "I am going to Italy, and I will take along anyone who wears the right clothes. I am wearing…" and describes their clothes.
- Players suggest outfits to wear, and the Leader says whether they can come along or not.
- The game continues until everyone guesses correctly.
- Secret: Describe the top half of the person on your right and the bottom half of the person on your left.

GIANT PICK UP STICKS

- Collect sticks about a foot in length.
- Hold all the sticks vertically together and then let go, releasing them into a random muddle onto the floor.
- Take it in turns declare which stick you will attempt to remove. After the deceleration, then attempt to remove said stick. This needs to be done without any other stick moving except the chosen one.
- If a stick moves other than the one they are

attempting to take out, then they forfeit their go, and it moves on to the next player.
- At the end of the game count everyones sticks. The person with the highest number wins.

STOMPING

- Use everyday items to create a short musical piece.
- Be imaginative with how you use the items, and keep the piece to around one minute.

SCISSORS

- Pass two sticks around a circle and say whether they are crossed or uncrossed.
- The leader tells the person if they are right or wrong.
- Secret: If the person's legs are crossed when they say "uncrossed," they are wrong, and vice versa.

POST-IT NOTE CHALLENGE

- Split into two teams, each choosing a person to be the mannequin (a camp councillor is a good choice!).
- On your command, teams stick post-it notes on their mannequin, one at a time.
- The first team to use all their post-it notes wins. Notes must be stuck individually, not in groups.
- If you don't have enough players to have a

mannequin then you can use a door or bunk bed instead.

MATCHBOX TASK

- Each player or team gets an empty matchbox.
- They have a set time to fill the matchbox with as many different items as possible. Items can only appear once in the matchbox.
- The player or team with the most items in their matchbox wins.

SHOOT, RELOAD

- Two people sit cross-legged opposite each other, slapping their knees and crossing their arms over their chest in time with each other.
- The aim is to "shoot" the other player. They need to know three gestures: shoot (two pointed fingers at their opponent in a gun gesture), reload (both thumbs back over their shoulder), and protect (cross arms across the chest).
- They can begin the processing of shooting at any time.
- Players must slap their knees between each gesture.
- To shoot, a player must first reload. Shooting at the same time as the other player or while they have their arms across their chest results in no score.
- The goal is to shoot when the opponent reloads, in which case you have won and can challenge the next player.

A-Z CONVO

- Have a conversation where each sentence starts with the next letter of the alphabet.
- If the group struggles, set a scene to make it easier.

60 SECOND CHALLENGE

- The whole group stands up and, after the person who is keeping time shouts "go", sits down when they think a minute has passed.
- The referee times them, and the person closest to 60 seconds wins. The person furthest away has a forfeit.

HAND JUDO

- Two friends challenge each other to Hand Judo. They stand facing each other about a metre apart. They should both hold their arms up, palms facing each other.
- The goal is to make the opponent lose their balance by pushing their hands.
- Moving feet to regain balance results in losing. Bow to your opponent after each point.

2 TRUTHS AND A LIE

- Take it in turns to go around the room, everyone declares three things about themselves. Two of those things are truths and one is a lie.
- Everyone else needs to try guess which is the lie.
- You can play again with different categories like pet peeves or bizarre situations.

THUMBMASTER

- Nominate a thumbmaster. If the thumbmaster places their thumb on the table(during a set period, everyone else must do the same. Everyone does this discretely so as not to give the game away.
- The last person to comply must do a forfeit and then becomes the next thumbmaster.
- This can be a good one to use at the dinner table to decide whose responsibility it is to clear up the plates at the end of the meal.

FINGER AIKIDO

- Players grip each other's hands with index fingers pointing out.
- Players must try touch the opponent with their index finger without breaking the grip or interfering with the other person.
- After each point, bow to your opponent before starting again.

BIRTHDAY ORDER

- On a command, everyone has to attempt to arrange themselves in a line by birthday order. January, on one end of the line, through to December, the other end of the line.
- This must be done without speaking.

TABOO

- A player is given a card with a word and several taboo words.
- They must describe the word without using any of the taboo words.
- The first person to guess correctly becomes the next player to receive a card.

QUIET DRAWINGS

- An artist is chosen and shown a scene to draw out of sight of the group.
- The artist returns and has five minutes to convey to their team what to draw, without speaking or pointing to items.
- The person with the most accurate picture wins and becomes the next artist.

DISTRACTION

- Players sit in pairs and discuss a topic for one minute.
- They then turn around and, once they can't see their opponent, are told to write down as many details about the other's clothing as they can remember.
- Compare notes and see who remembered the most.

POSTCARD TREASURE HUNT

- Cut a postcard into several pieces.
- Hide the pieces in a designated area.
- Everyone must rush to try to find the pieces and assemble the full postcard in as fast a time as possible.

HUMAN TANGLE

- Get all your friends to face each other.
- Everyone extends their right hand and grabs the hand of someone else.
- They then extend their left hand and grab a different person (so their left and right are holding on to different people).
- The challenge has been set - everyone needs to untangle themselves without letting go of anyones hands.
- For an added challenge, play a second time without talking.

EGG DROP

- Provide each group with an egg and craft materials.
- Give them 20 minutes to build a protective structure for the egg.
- Drop the egg from a second-floor window and see if it survives the fall.

NATURE SCAVENGER HUNT

- Split the group into two teams.
- Give them a list of items they need to find. The list needs to be things that they can find at camp - a toothbrush, a chewed leaf, 3 different size sticks - plus also include some general ideas - something smooth, something tiny, something prickly.
- Set a timer for 5 minutes.
- The team that collects the most items in the timeframe wins.

ORKY SNORKY

- Have your group sit in a circle.
- Choose one person to be "on" and blindfold them.
- Spin the blindfolded person around and have them point to someone.
- The blindfolded player says "Orky," and the person they are pointing to must reply "Snorky."
- The blindfolded player guesses who they think they are pointing to.

- If correct, they swap places; if wrong, the blindfolded player remains "on."

HEAD COUNT

- Have your group lie down on the floor and close their eyes.
- The group must count to 20, with each person saying one number at a time without any prior arrangement of order.
- If two people speak at the same time, the group must start over.

PASS THE GLASS

- Line up the group and blindfold them.
- Hand the first person a full glass of water and have them pass it down the line without spilling.
- Increase difficulty by creating an obstacle course or splitting into two teams and having a race.
- The team with the most water left in the glass at the end wins.

AFTER EIGHT CHALLENGE

- Each player places an After Eight chocolate on their forehead.
- The goal is to be the first to eat the chocolate without using their hands.

- The longer it takes, the more the chocolate melts, making for a hilarious game!

BLACK MAGIC

- Tell the group that you and a partner have a psychic connection.
- Send the partner out of the room while the group chooses an object.
- The partner returns, and you start asking, "Is it the white sheet? Is it the yellow ball? Is it the black ball?"
- The partner answers "no" to everything until you ask about a black item. The object named immediately after the black item is the chosen one.
- Alternatively, point at various coloured objects, and the object you point at after something black is the chosen one.
- See how long it takes everyone to work it out.

MAKING A KNOT

- Get someone to hold a piece of rope at both ends.
- Challenge your team to make a knot without letting go.
- Secret: Cross your arms before picking up the rope. Uncrossing your arms will create the knot.

RIGHT HAND CHALLENGE

- Ask everyone to put their right hand where their left hand can't reach.
- Secret: Place your right hand on your left elbow.

STACKING CUPS

- Place a long piece of string and three cups on a table.
- Challenge the group to stack the cups using the string without touching the cups.
- Secret: Create a loop around the cup with the string, twist it tightly in opposite directions, and use the string in this way to lift and stack the cups.

PSYCHIC POWERS

- Choose a volunteer and send them out of the room while the group selects a town or city.
- The volunteer returns and listens as the remaining person lists random towns or cities.
- When the chosen place is mentioned, the volunteer identifies it.
- Secret: The chosen place is always named right after "Manchester."

NUMBER STICKS

- Arrange sticks on the ground and ask what number they form.
- Everyone tries to guess the number.
- Secret: The number is determined by how many fingers you discreetly hold up.

HOW MANY FINGERS?

- Hold up different numbers of fingers and ask everyone to guess.
- Tell them if they are right or wrong until everyone has guessed the secret.
- The correct answer is always the number of fingers you held up before the current one.

CHAPTER 2
WOULD YOU RATHER? SUMMER CAMP EDITION

"Would You Rather?" is a classic summer camp game.

Players take turns asking each other questions that pose two different scenarios, and the person answering must choose which scenario they would prefer, while also stating their reasons 'why'.

The questions can range from thought-provoking to downright silly, encouraging lively discussions and lots of laughter.

Would you rather sleep in a bell tent in the rain or under the stars in warm weather?

Would you rather have a campfire an endless supply of marshmallows or a barbecue with an endless supply of hot dogs?

Would you rather go kayaking or rockclimbing?

Would you rather hike up the highest mountain on earth or visit the deepest cave on earth?

Would you rather swim in a lake or a swimming pool?

Would you rather have a picnic by the river or in a meadow?

Would you rather spend the night in a cabin infested with rats or a treehouse infested with cockroaches?

Would you rather catch fireflies or watch the stars?

Would you rather be a super fast swimmer but not able to run or be a super fast runner but not able to swim?

Would you rather go on a scavenger hunt or play capture the flag?

Would you rather make friendship bracelets or paint rocks?

Would you rather go on a night hike or have a night swim?

Would you rather eat s'mores every night or ice cream every afternoon?

Would you rather build a fort out of sticks or out of blankets?

Would you rather have a water balloon fight, where all the balloons are filled with strawberry milkshakes, or a mud fight, where all the mud is actually chocolate sauce?

Would you rather play volleyball for a whole day non-stop or soccer?

Would you rather go ziplining or rock climbing?

Would you rather make a craft or learn a new song?

Would you rather be visited by a ghost by the campfire or by a zombie in a cabin?

Would you rather have a campfire sing-along or a talent show?

Would you rather be a camp counselor or a camper?

Would you rather wear flip-flops that make an annoying squeaky noise when you walk or hiking boots that are really heavy?

Would you rather find a hidden treasure or discover a new trail?

Would you rather get lost in the woods in the middle of the day or have your tent collapse in the middle of the night?

Would you rather go to a camp dance or a camp movie night?

Would you rather have a campfire breakfast or a campfire dinner?

Would you rather see a bear or a snake in the wild?

Would you rather have a rainstorm or a heatwave during camp?

Would you rather paddle a canoe down a huge river with only one arm or be paddle a canoe down a huge river with someone singing 'this is the song that never ends' over and over?

Would you rather be the first to wake up or the last to go to bed?

Would you rather have a camp t-shirt or a camp hat as a souvenir?

Would you rather go to summer camp in England or in Paris?

Would you rather have a perfect campfire every night or the best swimming spot?

Would you rather go a whole year without snacks or a whole year without a phone?

Would you rather tell a scary story or hear one?

Would you rather have a talent for singing camp songs or telling camp jokes?

Would you rather go on a long hike or have a long nap?

Would you rather play the same summer camp game for 10 whole hours or sing different summer camp songs for 10 hours straight?

Would you rather always be the team leader or always be the last pick?

Would you rather cook your own meals at camp or have them prepared for you?

Would you rather see a beautiful sunset or a breathtaking sunrise?

Would you rather swim with fish or walk among wildflowers?

Would you rather learn to make a campfire or a shelter?

Would you rather be the best at archery or the best at swimming?

Would you rather have unlimited s'mores or unlimited hot chocolate?

Would you rather find a giant bug or get a small scratch from a thorn?

Would you rather explore the woods or relax by the campfire?

Would you rather always have sunscreen or always have bug spray?

Would you rather eat a wild berry you've never seen before or a mysterious dish from the camp kitchen?

Would you rather be known as the best storyteller or the best athlete at camp?

Would you rather sleep in a tent full of mice or sleep for a night with a sleeping porcupine as a pillow?

Would you rather sing every time you talk or dance every time you walk at camp?

Would you rather have to wear a small tent as a hat or huge flippers as shoes for a whole day?

Would you rather have twigs for hair or marshmallows for nails?

Would you rather always have to hop on one foot or crawl like a crab everywhere you go at camp?

Would you rather eat ice cream with sand in it or marshmallows with dirt in it?

Would you rather turn into a mosquito every night or a raccoon every morning?

Would you rather have a pet unicorn that snores really loud or a dragon that never stops talking?

Would you rather have to wear your swimsuit over your clothes or your clothes over your swimsuit all day?

Would you rather only be able to speak in campfire songs or whisper everything in a spooky ghost voice?

Would you rather be a tree that tells jokes or a rock that sings songs?

Would you rather have to eat s'mores for every meal or never eat s'mores again?

Would you rather always have to walk backwards or skip everywhere you go?

Would you rather be as small as an ant or as tall as a tree for a day at camp?

Would you rather have a talking sleeping bag or a tent that moves by itself?

Would you rather have to wear mittens on your feet or socks on your hands for a day?

Would you rather have a nose shaped like a mouth that repeats everything you say or ears shaped like noses that sneeze every time you talk?

Would you rather have to sing everything you say to the tune of "Happy Birthday" or "Twinkle, Twinkle Little Star"?

Would you rather find a spider in your sleeping bag or a frog in your boot?

Would you rather have to make friends with a bear or teach a fish to ride a bicycle?

Would you rather have a permanent itch on your nose or a constant tickle in your throat?

Would you rather have to eat a sandwich filled with bugs or drink a smoothie made of worms?

Would you rather have to howl at the moon every night or growl like a bear every morning?

Would you rather be a counselor's pet or a campfire's best friend?

Would you rather always smell like bug spray or sunscreen?

Would you rather always have sand in your shoes or always have water in your ears?

Would you rather eat your food with a shovel or with chopsticks made of licorice?

Would you rather have to wear floaties all the time or flippers everywhere you go?

Would you rather have to wear a snorkel in the shower or swim with your clothes on?

Would you rather have a magical marshmallow that never melts or a sleeping bag that never gets wet?

Would you rather be a ghost haunting the camp or an alien visiting the camp?

Would you rather always have to carry a giant pinecone or a heavy rock everywhere you go?

Would you rather have to wear a sleeping bag as a dress or a tent as a cape?

Would you rather always have to talk in a robot voice or sing like an opera singer?

Would you rather be the camp prankster or the camp mystery solver?

Would you rather have to hike wearing flip-flops or swim in your hiking boots?

Would you rather always have to wear a cape or always have to wear a silly hat?

Would you rather be a giant marshmallow or a tiny chocolate bar?

Would you rather have to eat cold soup or drink hot lemonade every day at camp?

Would you rather have to climb a tree to get to your bunk or swim across a pond?

Would you rather always only be able to talk in a shouting voice or in a whisper?

Would you rather have to sleep hanging from a tree like a bat or in a burrow like a rabbit?

Would you rather always have sticky fingers or wet socks?

Would you rather have to wear sunglasses at night or a headlamp during the day?

Would you rather be a camp counselor's shadow or a campfire's flame?

Would you rather freeze every time you hear music or dance every time there's silence?

Would you rather be covered in feathers or scales for a day?

Would you rather have to eat with your feet or drink through your ears?

Would you rather perform a silly dance in front of the whole camp or wear a ridiculous outfit for a whole day?

Would you rather receive a huge box full of sweets from home or have a day where the children get to tell the counselor's what to do (and they have to say yes!)?

CHAPTER 3

SUMMER CAMP JOKES

WHY DID the mushroom go to the party? *Because he was a fungi!*

What do you get when you cross a lake and a forest? *A tree-mendous splash!*

Why don't mountains get cold in the winter? *They wear snowcaps!*

What did the ocean say to the camper? *Nothing, it just waved!*

How do trees access the internet? *They log on!*

Why did the camper bring a ladder to the campground? *To climb to new heights!*

What do you call a sleeping bag that's been washed too many times? *A rip van wrinkle!*

How do bees get to school? *By the school buzz!*

What do you get if you cross a bear with a skunk? *Winnie the Phew!*

Why don't fish play basketball? *They're afraid of the net!*

What's a frog's favorite outdoor game? *Leapfrog!*

Why did the banana go to the campfire? *Because it wanted to be a s'more!*

Why don't ants get sick? *They have tiny ant-bodies!*

What do you call a dog that loves hiking? *A trail wagger!*

How do you organize a space camp party? *You planet!*

Why did the camper sit on a clock? *To be on time!*

What's a tree's favorite drink? *Root beer!*

Why did the squirrel swim across the river? *To get to the other side!*

What do you call a camp counselor who doesn't tell the truth? *A lyin' counselor!*

How do you know the ocean is friendly? *It waves!*

What do you get when you cross a cat with a camping lantern? *A cat-astrophe!*

Why don't trees take the bus? *They prefer to leaf!*

How do you throw a space party at camp? *You planet!*

What's a bear's favorite camp activity? *Bear-obics!*

What did the tree wear to the pool party? *Swimming trunks!*

How do mountains stay warm? *Snowcaps!*

Why don't birds use smartphones? *They prefer tweet-ment!*

What do you call a lazy camper? *A happy camper!*

Why did the campfire get in trouble? *It was always burning out!*

What did the river say to the camper? *Go with the flow!*

How do campers communicate in the forest? *They use tree-mail!*

What do you call a deer with no eyes? *No idea (no eye deer)!*

Why do fish avoid the computer at camp? *They don't want to get caught in the net!*

What do you call a sleeping dinosaur at camp? *A dino-snore!*

What's a chipmunk's favorite thing to draw? *Nut-ural landscapes!*

Why did the pine tree stay home from camp? *It had too many needles!*

What do you get when you cross a hammock and a parrot? *A polly-swing!*

Why don't rocks ever get lonely? *They have lots of boulder friends!*

What's a camp counselor's favorite type of tea? *Camp-anile tea!*

How do leaves get from place to place? *With autumn-mobiles!*

Why was the math book sad at camp? *It had too many problems!*

What did the tent say to the sleeping bag? *I've got you covered!*

What do you call a funny hiking story? *A trail-er tale!*

Why did the bat miss the campfire? *It was too busy hanging out!*

How do you stop a charging rhino? *Take away its credit card!*

What do you call a bear caught in the rain? *A drizzly bear!*

Why did the river start a band? *It had great flow!*

What do you call a camp counselor who loves to dance? *A camper-shaker!*

Why did the sun go to school? *To get a little brighter!*

How do you know if a tree is a dogwood tree? *By its bark!*

CHAPTER 4
SUMMER CAMP WRITING JOURNAL PROMPTS

Journaling is a wonderful way for you to capture your summer camp experiences, thoughts, and feelings.

Here are some engaging and fun prompts to use while you are journalling!

- **Arrival Day:** Describe your first day at camp. How did you feel when you arrived? What was the first thing you did?

- **Campfire Stories:** Write about a funny or scary story you heard around the campfire.

- **New Friends:** Describe someone new you met at camp. What makes them a good friend?

- **Favorite Activity:** What has been your favorite activity at camp so far? Why do you enjoy it?

- **Nature Walk:** Write about what you saw, heard, and felt during a nature walk. Did you discover anything interesting?

- **A Day in the Life:** Describe a typical day at camp from morning until bedtime.

- **Camp Food:** What is your favorite camp meal? Describe it in detail. Is there a meal you tried that you didn't like?

- **Funniest Moment:** What is the funniest thing that has happened at camp so far? Why was it so funny?

- **Overcoming Challenges:** Write about a challenge you faced at camp and how you overcame it.

- **Creative Campfire:** Imagine you could add any activity to camp. What would it be and why?

- **Animal Encounters:** Have you seen any animals at camp? Write about your encounter and how it made you feel.

- **Rainy Day:** What did you do during a rainy day at camp? How did you make the most of it?

- **Team Spirit:** Describe a time when you worked with other campers as a team. What did you accomplish together?

- **Camp Games:** Write about a game you played at camp. What were the rules, and who won?

- **Camp Counselor:** Describe your favorite camp counselor. What makes them special?

- **Night Sky:** Look up at the night sky and describe what you see. How do you feel when you look at the stars?

- **Letters Home:** Write a letter to your family about your camp experience. What would you tell them?

- **Craft Creations:** Describe a craft project you made. What materials did you use, and what did you create?

- **Adventure Story:** Write a short story about a camp adventure you'd like to have. Be as imaginative as you can!

- **Best Memory:** What has been the best moment of camp so far? Why is it your favorite memory?

CHAPTER 5
SMALL GROUP GAMES

THE GAMES in this chapter are perfect for small groups of 2-8 players.

They range from simple, quick-to-play activities to more complex, strategic games that test your thinking.

VEG, VEG, VEG

Number of Players: Minimum 4, no maximum

Equipment Needed: None

Objective: The player who is "on" must try to say another player's vegetable name three times in a row before the targeted player can say it once.

Setup: Each participant selects the name of a vegetable for themselves.

Rules:

1. The player who is "on" says another player's

vegetable name three times, e.g., "carrot, carrot, carrot."

2. If the targeted player fails to say their vegetable name once before the third repetition, they become "on."
3. If the targeted player says their vegetable name in time, the original "on" player remains and must try again with the same or a different vegetable.
4. Vegetables with longer syllables are more challenging, so players may switch vegetable names once they grasp the game.
5. The game can be played continuously and unexpectedly throughout the day, adding an element of surprise.

WHO AM I?

Number of Players: Minimum 3, no maximum

Equipment Needed: Post-it notes

Objective: Each player must figure out who or what they are.

Setup: Write a well-known name or object on a piece of paper and stick it to each player's forehead without them seeing it.

Rules:

1. Players can only ask yes or no questions for clues about their assigned name or object.
2. The game continues until every player has successfully identified their name or object.

LEG-GOALS

Number of Players: Minimum 6, no maximum

Equipment Needed: Football

Objective: Players protect their "goal" (the gap between their legs) while attempting to hit the ball through the goals of others in the circle.

Setup: Players form a circle, standing with their feet fairly wide apart and touching the feet of their neighbours on either side. Roll a football into the centre of the circle.

Rules:

1. Players bend forward and use their hands to protect their goal.
2. Each time a player concedes a goal, they lose a point and must put one arm behind their back.
3. After conceding another goal, the player turns around.
4. After a third goal, the player loses the use of their other arm.
5. If a player lets a fourth goal in, they are out of the game.
6. The last player standing is the winner.

MUMMY RELAY

Number of Players: Minimum 6, no maximum

Equipment Needed: Rolls of toilet paper

Setup: Divide everyone into teams with at least 3 players per team. Choose one member from each team to be the "mummy."

Objective: Teams race to wrap their mummy completely in toilet paper.

Rules:

1. On "go," the mummy stands with arms outstretched and legs apart.
2. The second team member wraps one of the mummy's legs.
3. The toilet paper is passed to the next player to wrap the other leg, then arms, and finally the body and head.
4. The first team to fully mummify their player wins.

HALT

Number of Players: Minimum 2, no maximum

Equipment Needed: None

Setup: Two players stand back to back and start walking away from each other at a signal.

Objective: The Challenger estimates the smallest number of strides needed to reach the other player.

Rules:

1. The pre-determined Challenger shouts "Halt!" at which point both players stop and turn around.
2. The Challenger estimates the number of strides needed to reach the other player.
3. The other player can either provide a lower estimate or say, "Prove it!"
4. If a lower number is offered, bidding continues until someone says, "Prove it!"

5. The player challenged to "prove it" must attempt to reach the other player in that number of steps.
6. If they succeed, they become the champion; if not, the other player wins.
7. The champion then faces a new challenger. This game can be played as an ongoing competition.

WATER BALLOON RACE

Number of Players: Minimum 2, no maximum

Equipment Needed: Water balloons (eco-reusable recommended)

Setup: Mark out a racecourse around 10 metres long. Add obstacles for more of a challenge if desired. Give each player a water balloon to hold between their legs.

Objective: Players race to the end of the track without bursting their water balloons.

Rules:

1. On "go," all players start racing to the end of the track.
2. If a balloon bursts, the player must return to the start to collect another one before beginning the course again.
3. The first player to finish with an intact water balloon wins.

FRENCH CRICKET

Number of Players: Minimum 5, no maximum

Equipment Needed: Cricket bat and ball

Setup: Players form a circle around one player who stands in the middle with a cricket bat.

Objective: The player in the middle defends their legs using only the cricket bat while the other players try to hit their legs with a tennis ball.

Rules:

1. The player in the middle must keep their feet together and cannot move.
2. The other players attempt to hit the player's legs below the knee with the tennis ball.
3. If a player hits the legs, they take the place of the player in the middle.
4. Players should maintain a reasonable distance to give the middle player a fair chance and only throw underarm.
5. Passing the ball between players is allowed.

TOWERBALL

Number of Players: Minimum 5, no maximum

Equipment Needed: Tennis ball, large cans

Setup: Stack two or three large cans to form a tower. Choose a player to become the 'guardian' of the tower. Everyone else then gathers in a circle around them.

Objective: The goal is to knock over the tower in full by throwing a tennis ball underarm, while the guardian's toys to protect the tower using only their legs and feet.

Rules:

1. Players in the circle can pass the ball among themselves before attempting to throw it at the tower.
2. When a player knocks over the tower, they become the new guardian. They must quickly rebuild the tower as the game continues during this transition.
3. A player also becomes the new guardian if they catch the ball after it rebounds off the current guardian.

HELLO!

Number of Players: Minimum 8, no maximum

Equipment Needed: None

Setup: Everone stands in a circle facing each other and one player is chosen to be 'on'.

Objective: The 'on' player walks around the outside of the circle and selects another player by touching them on the back, then races them to return to the same spot.

Rules:

1. The 'on' player touches another player on the back.
2. Both players then shake hands and run in opposite directions around the circle. (You can establish a rule that the first player continues in the direction they were walking, or they switch directions).
3. When they meet again, they shake hands a second time and then race to fill the gap left in the circle.
4. The player who fails to reach the gap first becomes the new 'on' player.

BAND-AID TAG

Number of Players: Minimum 7, no maximum

Equipment Needed: None

Objective: Play a game of tag with an added challenge.

Rules:

1. When a player is tagged, they must cover the spot where they were tagged with their hand, acting as a 'Band-Aid'.
2. If both hands are already being used as 'Band-Aids' and the player gets tagged again, they must go to the 'hospital' and are out of the game.
3. The game continues until only one player remains, who is declared the winner.

THROW IT & RUN

Number of Players: Minimum 8, no maximum

Equipment Needed: Tennis ball, cones or markers

Setup: Arrange a circle of cones or markers with one player designated as 'it' in the middle. The remaining players stand around the edge.

Objective: The player who is 'it' throws a tennis ball and attempts to tag as many players as possible before one of the outer players retrieves the ball and shouts "Stop!"

Rules:

1. 'It' throws the tennis ball and then tries to tag other players before the ball is picked up.

2. Once a player retrieves the ball and shouts "Stop!", the tagging must cease.
3. Any player who is tagged before "Stop!" is called must stand still and then join 'it' in the middle for the next round.
4. Only the original 'it' can throw the ball, but all players in the middle can tag others once the ball has been thrown.
5. Players around the edge can either try to save themselves by avoiding being tagged or attempt to reach the tennis ball to save their friends.

EARTH, AIR, WATER

Number of Players: Minimum 8, no maximum

Equipment Needed: Ball

Setup: Players sit or stand in a circle. The Leader stands in the middle holding a ball.

Objective: The Leader throws the ball to a player and calls out "Earth," "Air," or "Water." The player must catch the ball and quickly name a creature that lives in the specified environment before the Leader counts to three.

Rules:

1. The Leader throws the ball to any player while calling out "Earth," "Air," or "Water."
2. The receiving player must catch the ball and name a creature that inhabits the called environment before the Leader counts to three.
3. If the player fails to name a creature in time, they are out.

4. Players can't name the same animal more than once. If an animal is repeated, the player is out.
5. If a player misses the ball (as long as the throw is fair) then they are also out.

JUG HANDLED HE

Number of Players: Minimum 10, no maximum

Equipment Needed: None

Setup: Players pair off and link elbows. Each player's outer (non-linked) arm forms a 'jug handle' by placing the hand on their waist and holding the elbow out. One pair drops out, and one of them becomes 'on,' initiating the game by chasing the other member of their pair.

Objective: The player being chased can link elbows with any of the standing pairs to avoid being caught. When they link elbows, the other member of the linked pair becomes the new target.

Rules:

1. The player being chased can link elbows with any pair of standing players at any time.
2. When they link elbows, the other member of the standing pair must let go and becomes the new player being chased.
3. If the chaser catches the player being chased, their roles reverse, and the former chaser becomes the chased.
4. The new chased player can also link up with any pair at any time to continue the game, passing the role of being chased to another player.

CLAP BALL

Number of Players: Minimum 7, no maximum

Equipment Needed: Ball

Setup: Have the group stand in a circle and have a leader in the middle holding a ball.

Objective: Players must catch the ball after clapping once before catching it.

Rules:

1. The Leader throws the ball to a player in the circle.
2. The player must clap once before catching the ball.
3. A player is out if they fail to catch the ball, clap on a fake throw, or forget to clap.
4. The game continues until only one player remains, who is the winner.
5. To increase difficulty, players can be required to clap twice before catching the ball.

NAVIGATING TO THE MOON

Number of Players: Minimum 4, no maximum

Equipment Needed: Blindfolds, object to represent the moon

Setup: Select two players to be the 'rockets' and blindfold them. Choose two players to be the 'astronauts' who will remain in their place. Position the blindfolded rockets somewhere in the room. Mark out an area to be your 'space'. After the rockets are blindfolded, place a 'moon' somewhere in 'space'.

Objective: Astronauts must guide their rockets to land on the moon, or get as close as they can, using only verbal instructions.

Rules:

1. The first astronaut gives their rocket an instruction, specifying a number of paces and a direction.
2. The rocket follows the instruction in silence after it is given.
3. The second astronaut then gives their rocket an instruction, and the process alternates between the two astronauts, each giving up to three instructions in total.
4. The pair whose rocket is closest to the moon at the end of the instructions is the winning pair.

FIFTEEN PASSES

Number of Players: Minimum 6, no maximum

Equipment Needed: Ball

Setup: Split the group into two teams.

Objective: Players pass the ball around a designated area without the ball hitting the floor or being intercepted.

Rules:

1. Players must pass the ball to their teammates.
2. The first team to reach 15 consecutive passes without disruption wins.

BAD EGGS

Number of Players: Minimum 6, no maximum

Equipment Needed: Tennis ball

Setup: One player is 'on' and throws a tennis ball into the air, calling out the name of another player.

Objective: The player whose name is called must catch or fetch the ball, then try to hit another player.

Rules:

1. The catcher must shout 'STOP!' once they have the ball, and everyone must freeze.
2. The catcher specifies a player, takes a hop, skip, and jump in their direction, and throws the ball at them underarm.
3. If the target is hit, they become 'on' for the next round; otherwise, the catcher remains 'on'.
4. Players must keep still when being aimed at but can move the rest of their bodies to avoid being hit.

CHAIN HE

Number of Players: Minimum 8, no maximum

Equipment Needed: None

Setup: Players scatter in a designated area, and one player is 'on'.

Objective: The player who is 'on' tries to tag others, forming a chain with each player tagged.

Rules:

1. When a player is tagged, they join hands with the player who is 'on'.
2. The chain pursues other players, with new players joining the chain when tagged.
3. The game continues until all but one player is part of the chain.
4. Variation: Split the chains so there are no more than three players in a chain.

WORD HALT

Number of Players: Minimum 4, no maximum

Equipment Needed: List of words

Setup: Split the group into two teams and show one player from each team the same word.

Objective: Players must describe the word to their team within a limited number of words.

Rules:

1. Players guess how many words they can use to describe the word and challenge each other.
2. The player with the lowest bid attempts to describe the word to their team.
3. If the team guesses correctly, they score a point; if not, the other team scores.
4. The team with the most points at the end wins.

KEYWORDS

Number of Players: Minimum 4, no maximum

Equipment Needed: None

Setup: The group stands around the Leader, who chooses a keyword and tells a story.

Objective: Players must hide when the keyword is mentioned.

Rules:

1. When the keyword is mentioned, the group runs off to hide.
2. The Leader counts from ten to zero with eyes shut.
3. At zero, the Leader looks around and any visible player is out or loses a life.
4. This game is fun if played ongoing, so the Leader can catch the players out during mealtimes or other activities when they aren't ready.

BILL AND BOB

Number of Players: Minimum 6, no maximum

Equipment Needed: Rolled-up newspapers, blindfolds

Setup: Two players are blindfolded: one is 'Bill' and the other 'Bob'. They sit on the floor with left hands joined and each holding a rolled-up newspaper in their right hand.

Objective: Players try to tap the other lightly on the head with the newspaper.

Rules:

1. Bill asks, "Bob, are you there, Bob?" and Bob attempts to tap Bill.
2. A hit scores a point.
3. Bob then asks the equivalent question, and Bill tries to tap Bob.
4. Successful hits result in the player being swapped with someone else.

GRANDMOTHER'S FOOTSTEPS

Number of Players: Minimum 8, no maximum

Equipment Needed: None (optional: torch for variation)

Setup: One player is 'on' and stands some distance away, facing away from the rest of the group. The rest stand behind a starting line.

Objective: Players must stealthily advance and touch the 'on' player's back.

Rules:

1. While the ‘on’ player's back is turned, the others advance.
2. The ‘on’ player can turn around at any time, and anyone seen moving is sent back to the starting point.
3. The first player to touch the ‘on’ player's back wins and becomes 'on'.
4. Variation: Play in the dark with the ‘on’ player using a torch instead of turning around.

DRAGONS

Number of Players: Minimum 6, no maximum

Equipment Needed: Blindfolds

Setup:

1. Two teams stand in line, each person behind the other with their hands on the shoulders in front of them, forming a 'dragon'.
2. The front players of each dragon are blindfolded.

Objective: The blindfolded player must touch the rearmost member of the opposing dragon.

Rules:

1. The players behind guide the blindfolded player by tapping their shoulders to move left or right.
2. The dragons must not break their hold.
3. No verbal instructions are allowed.

HEAD THE CATCH

Number of Players: Minimum 6, no maximum

Equipment Needed: Ball

Setup: Players stand side by side facing the Leader, who is about 5 metres away.

Objective: Players must correctly follow the Leader's commands to either head or catch the ball.

Rules:

1. The Leader throws the ball to a player and shouts "Head!" or "Catch!"
2. The player must either header or catch the ball as instructed.
3. After a few successful tries, reverse the commands: "Head!" means catch and "Catch!" means header.
4. Add "Knee" and "Elbow" as additional commands for more challenge.
5. The game can be played with forfeits or as an elimination game to find a winner.

CHINESE TUG OF WAR

Number of Players: Minimum 2, no maximum

Equipment Needed: None

Setup: Two contestants stand back to back and grasp left hands between their legs.

Objective: Contestants attempt to reach a mark placed a suitable distance in front of them.

Rules:

1. At "Go!", both players try to reach their respective marks.
2. The first player to reach their mark wins and stays on to face a new player.
3. Continue the game with new challengers as long as desired.

---

10 SECONDS

Number of Players: Minimum 4, no maximum

Equipment Needed: None

Setup: The Leader stands ready to give commands.

Objective: Players must follow the Leader's commands within 10 seconds.

Rules:

1. The Leader shouts out a command and counts down from 10.
2. Anyone who doesn't follow the command within the time limit is out.
3. Examples of commands: Sit in a circle, Touch something blue, Stand in groups of 5, Touch someone whose name begins with a specific letter.
4. The game continues until only one player remains, who is the winner.

REBELLIOUS SIMON

Number of Players: Minimum 4, no maximum

Equipment Needed: None

Setup: Players sit in a circle with the Leader in the middle.

Objective: Players must perform the opposite actions of what the Leader does.

Rules:

1. If the Leader stands, players must sit.
2. If the Leader sits, players must stand.

3. When the Leader raises their arms, players must lower theirs.
4. When the Leader lowers their arms, players must raise theirs.

BLINDFOLDED SHOE SHUFFLE

Number of Players: Minimum 4, no maximum

Equipment Needed: Blindfolds, shoes

Setup: Each player takes off their shoes and throws them into a pile before putting on a blindfold.

Objective: Players must find their own shoes by touch alone and put them on.

Rules:

1. The referee jumbles up the shoe pile.
2. At the signal "GO!", players search for their shoes using only their sense of touch.
3. The first player to find and put on their shoes wins.

HEAD OR TAILS

Number of Players: Minimum 4, no maximum

Equipment Needed: Coin

Setup: Everyone stands in a circle.

Objective: Players must guess whether a coin will land on heads or tails.

Rules:

1. Players choose heads or tails by placing their hands on their heads or bottoms.
2. Flip a coin and announce the result.
3. Players who chose the wrong option are out.
4. Continue until only one player remains, who is the winner.

SCREAMING SHOES

Number of Players: Minimum 8, no maximum

Equipment Needed: None

Setup: Players stand in a circle, focusing on one person's shoes.

Objective: Players try to avoid eye contact with the same person at the same time.

Rules:

1. The Leader counts to three.
2. On "three," everyone looks up and chooses one person to look at.
3. If two players catch each other's gaze, they scream and sit out.
4. Continue until only one player remains or everyone is out simultaneously.

HIDDEN SURPRISE

Number of Players: Minimum 4, no maximum

Equipment Needed: Empty pill bottle, money or sweets, newspaper, various tapes, dice

Setup: Place money or sweets in an empty pill bottle and wrap it with layers of newspaper and various tapes, forming a ball. Players stand in a circle with a set of dice.

Objective: Players try to unwrap the tape ball to reach the hidden surprise.

Rules:

1. Players take turns rolling the dice.
2. If a player rolls a double, they enter the circle and start unwrapping the ball.
3. The unwrapping continues until another player rolls a double.
4. The player who reaches the hidden surprise wins and keeps it.

PIRATE

Number of Players: Minimum 8, no maximum

Equipment Needed: Blindfold, keys on a keyring

Setup: Choose one player to be the pirate and blindfold them. The pirate sits in the middle of the circle. Place several rings of keys in front of the pirate or under their chair.

Objective: Players try to steal a ring of keys without being detected by the pirate.

Rules:

1. Players sit in a circle with legs crossed.
2. One player is nominated to creep up and attempt to take a ring of keys.
3. The pirate has three chances to point in the direction of the thief.

4. If the thief succeeds, they become the new pirate. If not, a different player gets a turn.

PIP POP

Number of Players: Minimum 8, no maximum

Equipment Needed: Ball

Setup:

1. Players sit or stand in a circle with the Leader standing in the middle holding a ball.

Objective: Players must respond with the opposite phrase to what the Leader says as quickly as possible.

Rules:

1. If the Leader says "Pip" to a player, the player must respond with "Pop."
2. If the Leader says "Pip Pop," the player must respond with "Pop Pip."
3. The response to "Pop Pip Pop" is "Pip Pop Pip," and so on, always replying with the opposite sequence.
4. The Leader addresses players rapidly around the circle.
5. Any player who makes a mistake is out and must sit out of the game.
6. The last player remaining is the winner.

CHAPTER 6
LARGE GROUP GAMES

This section is dedicated to summer camp games ideally played with larger groups of 12+ participants.

Ideal for getting competitive and playing against other cabins!

COMBAT

Equipment Needed: Combat cards, whistle/bell, cricket stumps

Setup:

1. Split the group into teams of ten (or adjust as needed).
2. Each team receives the following cards: Field Marshall (50 pts), General (10 pts), Colonel (9 pts), Major (8 pts), Captain (7 pts), Lieutenant (6 pts), Sergeant (5 pts), Corporal (4 pts), and two Spies (1 pt each). Adjust ranks as needed while keeping the Field Marshall and both Spies.
3. Each team sets up a camp marked with a cricket

stump. Distribute cards either randomly or strategically.

Objective: Capture all opponents by taking them prisoner.

Rules:

1. On the starting signal, players leave their camps to challenge opponents by touching them.
2. Players compare cards, and the higher rank wins, except the Field Marshall is beaten by a Spy.
3. If players of the same rank challenge each other, neither is captured.
4. The winner takes the loser as a prisoner to their camp. The first prisoner holds the cricket stump, and subsequent prisoners form a line.
5. Prisoners can be freed by a teammate tagging the end of the line before being challenged.
6. The game ends when one team captures all opponents or holds the highest points value of prisoners when the whistle blows.
7. Players cannot challenge or be challenged in their own camp or while escorting a prisoner.
8. Variation: The game can end when one team captures the Field Marshall, allowing for shorter games and more strategic play.

NEWSPAPERS

Equipment Needed: Newspapers, chairs, writing materials

Setup:

1. Provide each team with the same copy of a newspaper.

2. Arrange three chairs labeled first, second, and third at the front of the room.

Objective: Answer questions based on the newspaper content and complete challenges for points.

Rules:

1. The Leader asks a question, and teams search the newspaper for the answer.
2. Teams race to sit in the chairs based on their position (first, second, third) and write down the answer.
3. Correct answers earn points according to the chair position; incorrect answers allow the next team to guess.
4. After a few questions, each team completes a challenge using the newspaper (e.g., make a paper airplane, build a tower, create an outfit).
5. Teams earn extra points for the best performances in challenges.
6. Continue with more questions, noting that damaged newspapers make it harder.
7. The team with the most points at the end wins.
8. To ensure participation, the Leader can specify which team member must give the answer.

DUTCH AUCTION

Equipment Needed: Suitcases or bags, various random objects

Setup:

1. Give each team a set amount of time to fill a suitcase with random objects.

2. Teams sit with their suitcases at the front of the room with chairs labeled first, second, and third.

Objective: Use random objects to match descriptions given by the Leader.

Rules:

1. The Leader calls for an item (e.g., "something to make me look pretty").
2. Teams search their suitcase and run to sit in the chairs based on their position.
3. Teams explain why their item fits the description. Creativity is encouraged.
4. The judge awards points based on the explanation.
5. Repeat with various items, with a good final item being "a pillowcase".
6. The winning team is the one with the highest number of points at the end of play.
7. To ensure participation, the Leader can specify which team member must present the item.

PICTIONARY

Equipment Needed: Whiteboards or paper, markers

Setup:

1. Teams sit together.

Objective: Guess the word based on a teammate's drawing.

Rules:

1. Each team sends one member to the Leader to receive a word (book, object, or film).

2. The player draws the word without speaking or writing words, and their team guesses.
3. The first team to guess correctly wins a point.
4. Alternatively, use a single board visible to all teams and have one player draw for everyone.
5. Teams can put up their hand to guess. Correct guesses earn a point; incorrect guesses allow play to continue.
6. Each team gets one guess per round.
7. The team with the most points at the end wins.

CATEGORIES

Equipment Needed: Paper, pens

Setup:

1. Divide players into small teams of 4-8.
2. Provide each team with a list of categories (e.g., boys/girls names, countries, animals, fruit, clothing items).

Objective: Come up with words that fit the given categories and start with the specified letter.

Rules:

1. At the beginning of each round, give teams a letter and 1 minute to write a word for each category starting with that letter.
2. Correct answers earn 5 points each. Duplicate answers with other teams earn 1 point.
3. The team with the most points at the end wins.

SNAKES & LADDERS

Equipment Needed: Snakes and ladders board, dice, numbered questions

Setup:

1. Set up a room or area with 52 numbers hidden in different places, each with a question behind it.
2. Have a question keeper with a snakes and ladders board and dice.

Objective: Navigate the snakes and ladders board by answering questions correctly.

Rules:

1. Teams take turns rolling the dice and moving on the snakes and ladders board.
2. They must find the corresponding number, read the question, and answer it.
3. Correct answers allow them to roll again. Incorrect answers give them another guess, and if still wrong, they must do a forfeit.
4. Landing on a ladder moves them up; landing on a snake moves them down.
5. The last team to reach the end wins.

---

4 COLOURS

Equipment Needed: Coloured markers for corners (red, blue, green, yellow)

Setup:

1. Clear a room and place markers in each corner to represent different colours.

Objective: Move to the correct coloured corner as quickly as possible.

Rules:

1. Players mill around the room until the Leader shouts a colour.
2. Players run to the corresponding corner and form a queue.
3. The last few players in the queue are out.
4. Continue until one winner remains.

HOCKEY BY NUMBERS

Equipment Needed: Chairs, rolled-up newspapers, football

Setup:

1. Separate players into two equal teams and sit them in rows facing each other.
2. Give each player a number on each side, so they have a matching number sat across from them.
3. Place a chair (which will act as your goal) with a rolled-up newspaper (which will act as your hockey stick) at the end of each row. Place a football in the middle.

Objective: Score goals by hitting the football into the opponent's goal using the newspaper hockey stick.

Rules:

1. The leader calls out a number. Those players then jump up, grab their hockey stick and try to score by putting the ball through their goal.
2. The Leader can shout a new number at any point. They current players drop their hockey stick where they are and return to their places - the new players pick up where the others left off.
3. The team with the most goals at the end wins.
4. As the game goes on, the hockey sticks get worn and harder to use adding to the fun.

WINKING GAME

Equipment Needed: Chairs

Setup:

1. Half the group sits in a circle on chairs (sitters), while the other half stands behind each chair (standers), except for one player who is 'on' and stands behind an empty chair.

Objective: The 'on' player must get a sitter to move to the empty chair by winking at them.

Rules:

1. The 'on' player winks at a sitter, who must then quickly move to the empty chair.
2. The stander behind the sitter tries to prevent them from moving by placing their hands on the sitter's shoulders.
3. If the sitter escapes, they move to the empty chair, and their stander becomes the new 'on' player.

4. If the sitter is stopped, they sit back down, and the 'on' player tries again.

ANIMAL SOUNDS

Equipment Needed: Animal cards

Setup:

1. Create groups of animal cards, mix them up, and give one to each player.

Objective: Find other players with the same animal card using only animal sounds.

Rules:

1. At the signal, players look at their card and start making the corresponding animal sound.
2. Players must find others making the same sound.
3. The first team to find all their members wins.

LADDERS

Equipment Needed: None

Setup:

1. Divide the group into two equal teams and have them sit facing each other with legs stretched out, touching the feet of their opponents.
2. Number each player from top to bottom so that corresponding numbers face each other.

Objective: Race to complete the course and score points for the team.

Rules:

1. The Leader calls a number, and the corresponding players run to the end of the line, back around to the top, and sit in their original place.
2. The first player back scores a point for their team.
3. The team with the most points at the end wins.

BLIND MAN'S BUFF

Equipment Needed: Blindfold

Setup:

1. Clear the room by pushing all chairs and tables out of the way.
2. Choose one player to be "Buff" and blindfold them.

Objective: The blindfolded player (Buff) tries to catch and identify another player.

Rules:

1. The other players ask Buff, "How many horses has your father got?" Buff replies, "Three." Then they ask, "What colour are they?" Buff responds, "Black, white, and grey."
2. Everyone calls out, "Turn around three times and catch whom you may."
3. Buff turns around and tries to catch another player.
4. Once a player is caught, Buff must guess who it is before removing the blindfold.

5. If Buff guesses correctly, the caught player becomes the new Buff. If not, Buff continues.

KICK THE CAN (LURKY)

Equipment Needed: Can

Setup:

1. Draw a circle in the middle of a flat area and place a can upside down in the centre.
2. Choose one player to be the keeper of the can.

Objective: Players hide while the keeper seeks and makes them prisoners by identifying their location.

Rules:

1. The keeper shuts their eyes and counts to 30 while the others run and hide.
2. The keeper must searches for the other players. If they spot anyone they make them prisoner by returning them to the can, placing a foot on it, and calling out "lurky….." followed by the person's name (or a description of what they're wearing if everyone isn't familiar with names yet) , plus the location.
3. Prisoners must be honest - if called out, they return go to the can. The first prisoner must have a foot touching the can, and the second just needs to be touching the first prisoner so they can stretch out and make a long line, improving their chances of being freed.
4. To free the prisoners, other players can either kick the can (before the keeper catches them out), or tags the

prisoner at the end of the line (before the keeper catches them out).
5. The keeper wins when all players are caught and made prisoners.
6. The last to be caught becomes the new keeper.

PRISONER BALL

Equipment Needed: Ball, field markers

Setup:

1. Mark out a field with two square spaces for each team.
2. Teams stand in their designated spaces facing each other with a ball in play.

Objective: Hit opponents with the ball to make them prisoners while avoiding getting hit.

Rules:

1. Players throw the ball at opponents, aiming below the neck. The ball must not hit the ground first.
2. If a player is hit, they become a prisoner and move behind the opponent's field.
3. Prisoners can throw the ball from behind the opponent's field to free themselves if they hit an opponent.
4. Inter-passing between players and prisoners is allowed.
5. The team with the last player standing wins.

BENCHBALL

Equipment Needed: Benches, ball

Setup:

1. Split the group into two teams with a bench at each end of the pitch.
2. Each team has one goalie on their bench.

Objective: Score by passing the ball to the goalie without it being intercepted.

Rules:

1. Players throw the ball to each other but cannot move while holding the ball.
2. The goalie on each bench can catch the ball and pass it back into play.
3. To score, a player must pass the ball to the goalie. If successful, the player joins the goalie on the bench.
4. The game ends when all players are on the bench.

SUITS

Equipment Needed: Deck of cards

Setup:

1. Everyone sits in a circle on chairs.
2. The leader distributes a card to each player from a shuffled deck, who must remember their suit.

Objective: Move around the circle and be the first to return to the starting seat.

Rules:

1. The leader collects and reshuffles the cards.
2. The leader picks the top card from the deck and calls out its suit.
3. All players with that suit move one space to the left, sitting on the person's lap if necessary.
4. If a player cannot move because someone is on their lap, they stay put.
5. The first player to make it all the way around the circle back to their starting seat wins.

BOAT RACE

Equipment Needed: None

Setup:

1. Divide players into teams, each forming a 'crew' lined up facing backwards with hands on the shoulders of the person in front.
2. One team member is the 'cox' and stands at the back, facing forward.

Objective: Be the first team to reach a marker, turn around, and return.

Rules:

1. On "Go!", crews race to a marker about 50 metres away, round it, and return.
2. Teams must remain linked by hands on shoulders at all times.
3. Any team that breaks the link must return to the start, re-link, and set off again.

4. The first team back wins.

HAWK

Equipment Needed: None

Setup:

1. One player is chosen to be the 'hawk', and the remaining players line up at one end as the 'deer'.

Objective: The hawk tries to catch the deer as they run across the field.

Rules:

1. When the hawk is ready, the deer run from one end of the playing area to the other.
2. The hawk tries to tag the deer. Tagged deer become 'wings' and help the hawk catch other deer.
3. Only the hawk's tag counts for catching deer.
4. Wings can split off and operate singly or in pairs but cannot use their arms to hold the deer.
5. The last deer caught becomes the new hawk.

JOCKEYS

Equipment Needed: None

Setup:

1. Players form pairs and stand in a circle, with one member (the jockey) on the other's back.
2. Place an object in the middle of the circle.

Objective: Score points by being the first jockey to grab the object in the centre.

Rules:

1. The leader calls "Right!" or "Left!".
2. The jockeys dismount, race around the circle in the called direction, and dive between their partner's legs.
3. The first jockey to grab the object scores a point for their pair.
4. The jockeys and mounts change roles regularly.
5. The first pair to reach a prearranged number of points wins.

TWINS

Equipment Needed: None

Setup:

1. Everyone gets into pairs. Stand in a circle, holding the hands of your partner.
2. One pair is chosen as "it" and become the runners.

Objective: Tag a pair of joined hands and race to occupy their spot.

Rules:

1. The pair that is 'it' walks around the outside of the circle and tag a pair.
2. The tagged pair and the runners race in opposite directions around the circle.
3. The pair to reach the vacated spot first wins, and the other pair becomes "it".

LINE & FIELDERS

Equipment Needed: Football

Setup:

1. Divide players into two teams: one batting, one fielding.
2. The batting team stands in a line, one behind the other. The fielding team scatters on the field.

Objective: Score runs by completing circuits while the fielding team retrieves the ball.

Rules:

1. The first batter throws or kicks the ball as far as possible.
2. The batter runs around the batting team, counting each circuit as a run.
3. The fielding team retrieves the ball and passes it overhead until it reaches the last fielder.
4. The last fielder shouts "Stop!" and the batter stops running.
5. Each player on the batting team takes a turn.
6. Teams switch roles after all have batted.
7. The team with the highest total runs wins.

HORSE SHOE

Equipment Needed: Blindfolds, cups

Setup:

1. Everyone sits in a circle.
2. Two players are blindfolded and seated in chairs (horses) placed in the circle.
3. Place eight empty cups around the inside of the circle.

Objective: Be the first player to put all four cups on the legs of their chair and sit down.

Rules:

1. On "Go!", the blindfolded players feel their way to the cups.
2. Players must place a cup on each leg of their chair.
3. The first player to get all four cups on and sit down wins.
4. The other players can shout directions to help but cannot touch the cups.

SCOTS & ENGLISH

Equipment Needed: Football goals or markers for prisons, six tennis balls or tokens per team

Setup:

1. Designate a large playing area with a prison at each end.
2. Spread six tennis balls or other tokens evenly along each end line.
3. Divide the field into two halves, one for each team.

Objective: Capture all the treasure from the opponent's end line or rescue prisoners.

Rules:

1. Players may cross the centre line to enter the opponent's territory and attempt to capture a piece of treasure.
2. Players can be tagged by opponents once they cross the centre line, becoming prisoners.
3. Prisoners are escorted to the opponent's prison by their captor.
4. Captors may not tag another player until their prisoner is in prison.
5. Players reaching the opponent's end line without being tagged can either take a piece of treasure or release a prisoner by tagging them.
6. Released prisoners and players with treasure are invulnerable while returning to their side.
7. The game is won when one team has all the treasure on their own end line.

SKINNING THE SNAKE

Equipment Needed: None

Setup:

1. Split everyone into teams - get them to line up one behind the other.
2. Players puts their left hand back between their legs and their right hand forward to hold the left hand of the player in front.

Objective: Crawl through the legs of teammates and reform the line without breaking hands.

Rules:

1. On "Go!", the player at the end of the 'snake' crawls through the legs of the player in front.
2. Each subsequent player follows through the tunnel until everyone is through and standing again.
3. Hands must not be broken at any time.
4. Teams can race or demonstrate agility.
5. Variation: Players can simply reach backwards with their left hands, not through the legs, for a slightly easier version.

BOMBING

Equipment Needed: Ball, markers for square

Setup:

1. Mark out a square on the ground.
2. All players stand inside the square.
3. Two players stand outside the square, one on each side.

Objective: Avoid being hit by the ball thrown by the players outside the square.

Rules:

1. The two players outside the square throw the ball at those inside, passing between themselves if desired.
2. Any player hit below the waist must join the throwers outside the square.
3. The last player remaining inside the square wins.

FISHING

Equipment Needed: Newspaper fish shapes, string

Setup:

1. Cut out fish shapes from newspaper and attach strings to their noses.
2. Players tie the strings to their waists so the fish touch the ground behind them.

Objective: Tread on other players' fish while keeping your own intact.

Rules:

1. On the signal to start, players try to step on the fish of other players to detach them.
2. Players dodge and avoid getting their fish stepped on.
3. The last player with an intact fish wins.
4. Can be played with two players at a time or with everyone at once.

SOMEONE MOVED

Equipment Needed: None

Setup:

1. All players sit in a circle.
2. Choose one player to be "it" and have them leave the room.

Objective: Identify the players who moved in the circle.

Rules:

1. While "it" is out of sight, one to four players move positions in the circle.
2. "It" returns and tries to figure out who moved.
3. The game continues with different players being "it".

ARTFUL DODGER

Equipment Needed: None

Setup:

1. Players stand in a circle.
2. Choose two players to be "keepers" and one to be the "dodger".

Objective: The dodger must avoid being tagged by the keepers.

Rules:

1. The dodger runs around two standing players (one at a time) without being tagged by either keeper.
2. Keepers cannot enter the circle, so the dodger is safe except when running around a standing player.
3. If the dodger succeeds, they return to their original place, and the next person clockwise becomes the dodger.
4. If the dodger is tagged, they switch places with the keeper who tagged them.
5. The game continues until everyone has had a turn as the dodger.
6. Adjust the number of keepers and dodgers to suit the number of players.

CHAPTER 7
CAMPFIRE RIDDLES

1. What has a neck but no head, two arms but no hands?

———

2. What has a head, a tail, is brown, and has no legs?

———

3. What can you hold in your left hand but not in your right?

———

4. What has a bottom at the top?

———

5. What has words but never speaks?

———

6. What is so light, even the smallest child can hold it for long?

———

7. What starts with P, ends with E, and has thousands of letters?

———

8. What kind of room has no doors or windows?

———

9. What is always coming but never arrives?

———

10. What is easy to get into, but hard to get out of?

———

11. What has many teeth but can't bite?

———

12. What can be cracked, made, told, and played?

———

13. What is cut on a table, but never eaten?

———

14. What has an eye but cannot see, and is faster than any man alive?

———

15. What has legs, but doesn't walk?

———

16. What has a spine but no bones?

———

17. What has four eyes but can't see?

———

18. What can run but never walks, has a mouth but never talks?

———

19. What goes through cities and fields, but never moves?

———

20. What can be broken without being held?

———

21. What has keys that open no locks, with space but no room, and you can enter but not go inside?

———

22. What can you keep after giving to someone?

———

23. What has many keys but can't open any doors?

______

24. What has a ring but no finger?

______

25. What is always in front of you but can't be touched?

______

26. What is black when it's clean and white when it's dirty?

______

27. What flies without wings?

______

28. What goes up and down but doesn't move?

______

29. What has cities without houses, rivers without water, and forests without trees?

______

30. What is something you will never see again?

______

31. What has a head, a tail, is brown, and has no legs?

______

32. What comes down but never goes up?

33. What can be seen once in a minute, twice in a moment, and never in a thousand years?

34. What is always in front of you but can't be seen?

35. What is so delicate that saying its name breaks it?

36. What is full of holes but still holds water?

37. What can travel around the world while staying in one corner?

38. What has one eye but can't see?

39. What begins with an "E" but only has one letter in it?

40. What goes up and never comes down?

RIDDLE ANSWERS

1 A SHIRT

2 A penny

3 Your right elbow

4 A leg

5 A book

6 A breath

7 A post office

8 A mushroom

9 Tomorrow

10 Trouble

11 A comb

12 A joke

13 A deck of cards

14 A needle

15 A table

16 A book

17 Mississippi (the state or the river, known for its four 'i's)

18 A river

19 A road

20 A promise

21 A keyboard

22 Your word

23 A piano

24 A telephone

25 The future

26 A chalkboard

27 Time

28 A staircase

29 A map

30 Yesterday

31 A penny

32 Rain

33 The letter "M"

34 The future

35 Silence

36 A sponge

37 A stamp

38 A needle

39 An envelope

40 Your age

CHAPTER 8
CAMPFIRE CONVERSATIONS

USE these conversation starters to get to know your fellow campers better. You might also discover some new things about yourself.

These are perfect to use when sat around the campfire, when on walks, or having downtime in your cabins.

What's your favourite part of summer camp?

If you could have any superpower, what would it be and why?

What's the best book you've ever read?

If you could visit any place in the world, where would you go?

What's your favourite animal and why?

What's the most fun thing you've ever done?

If you could be any character from a movie or TV show, who would you be?

What's your favourite campfire snack?

Do you have a favourite joke or riddle?

What's the coolest thing you've learned at school recently?

If you could have any pet, what would it be?

What's your favourite outdoor activity?

Have you ever seen a shooting star? What did you wish for?

———

What's the most interesting place you've ever visited?

———

If you could only eat one food for the rest of your life, what would it be?

———

What's your favourite game to play with friends?

———

Do you know any ghost stories?

———

What's something you're really good at?

———

If you could meet any famous person, who would it be and why?

———

What's your favourite subject in school?

———

What's the best gift you've ever received?

If you could time travel, where would you go?

Do you have any special talents or skills?

What's the funniest thing that's ever happened to you?

What's your favourite song to sing along to?

If you could invent something, what would it be?

What's the best advice you've ever received?

Do you have a favourite family tradition?

If you were a superhero, what would your name be?

What's your favourite thing about nature?

Do you have any dreams for the future?

What's your favourite holiday and why?

If you could swap places with anyone for a day, who would it be?

What's your favourite colour and why?

Have you ever had a really funny dream? What was it about?

If you could create a new animal, what would it look like and what would it be called?

What's the best prank you've ever played on someone?

Do you have a favourite campfire song?

What's something you want to learn how to do?

If you found a magic lamp and had three wishes, what would you wish for?